Silhouettes in the Electric Sky

The best poetry from two years
of *Gravity: A Journal of
Online Writing*

Silhouettes in the Electric Sky

The best poetry from two years
of *Gravity: A Journal of Online Writing*

http://www.newtonsbaby.com/gravity/

Edited and Introduced by John Carle

Newton's Baby, Atlanta

Anthology Copyright 1998 John Carle

Newton's Baby
788 Murphey Street
Scottdale, GA 30079

First Edition, November 1998

Library of Congress Catalog Card Number: 98-96655

ISBN: 0-9667228-0-9

Cover design and art by Cheryl Hight Carle

Printed in Canada

Contents

7

Art Credits

Introduction

The poets whose work is represented in this anthology are a diverse bunch. Most are American, but there are writers here from Germany, Canada and Australia as well. They work as construction foremen, shop owners, pub-lishers, teachers, computer gurus, students and parents. Their poems follow no one style or school of thought and, unless you have followed *Gravity* or other online litzines, you've probably never heard of many of them.

All of them tell stories, some imagined and some from life, and this has been one of the exciting things about publishing on the Internet - the wider avail-ability of publishing outlets to poets writing outside the university journals or *American Poetry Review*. That's the closest *Gravity* comes to having an ethic, the idea that we're better off telling each other our stories. It's something that happens every day on the 'net, from Ian Irvine's *The Animist* to Jennifer Ley's *Perihelion*.

Gravity is proud to have been a part, however small, of that community of publishers. The 'zine itself wouldn't have happened without the high caliber of poetry sent in since July, 1996, so first thanks go to the writers for their support. The idea for, and initial advice concerning, this book came from Caron Andregg, whose annual Poetry Calendar had published many of the poets you'll read here. Jolie Simmons provided generous technical assistance, while Chuck deVarennes and Dave Sloan graciously let me get on my soapbox at their Lonesome Virgin reading to sell this thing to the hometown crowd. Betty Curnutt essentially underwrote a third of this project. I am indebted to all these, but to none so much as to my wife Cheryl, who designed the cover and put up with me while this book was in production.

Look for another volume in two years.

John Carle
Atlanta, October 1998

Suggested Further Reading

Aabye's Baby http://www.geocities.com/Paris/Cafe/9091/

Agnieszka's Dowry http://www.enteract.com/~asgp/agnieszka.html

The Animist http://www.diskotech.com.au/asphodel/

The Astrophysicist's Tango Partner Speaks http://www.heelstone.com

Conspire http://www.msu.edu/~towerchr/conspire/

CrossConnect http://tech1.dccs.upenn.edu/~xconnect/

Mind Fire http://www.geocities.com/~mind-fire/

Morpo Review http://www.morpo.com/

Perihelion http://www.webdelsol.com/Perihelion/

The Poetry Cafe http://www.poetrycafe.com/

Recursive Angel http://www.calldei.com/~recangel/index1.html

Spoken War http://www.spokenwar.com/

Thunder Sandwich http://www.geocities.com/SoHo/Cafe/7475/

Tintern Abbey http://home.earthlink.net/~tannlund/

Web del Sol http://www.webdelsol.com/

Zero City http://www.cruzio.com/~zerocity/

Zuzu's Petals http://www.zuzu.com/

Perry Thompson

My Mother Whistled the Sunday News

My mother whistled the Sunday news
by a stream where all the trout knew her music.

Horses cut in soap and afternoons of cinnamon
laughter were my inheritance.

Banks stole the rest.

My mother loved the clouds -- a silhouette of Mark
Twain here, Sitting Bull's rocking chair over there.

My mother had visions. She heard voices.
They told her love's the rainy season of your life.

But gentlemen bloomed when mother's melodies
opened one laughing petal at a time

their dry hearts. My mother's gentlemen
curled about her spirit self like smoke

from the peace pipe of ancient families
going to silhouettes in the slippery sky.

One of these men stayed. I was his also.
My father sang the Sunday news.

We Lay War

we lay war
dead shoulder
to shoulder in blank
friendship,
line graveyards
in perfect rows
as if to confound
death with our preciseness.

startled by the carrion's blue
and winking eye
the child wonders
if this is how the hero feels,
sickened at the orange
taste of blood,
its warm way of covering
the hands and feet.

and when the hero
in his blonde blood
comes before
the child for execution,
old men draw near
to whisper lies
that fill the ear
and stay the hand.

in perfect rows
the soldiers pass,
parades the child can learn
to march in,
machinery precise
complete with young girls
dressed in black
with dark blank eyes.

A Saint Dreamed She Died and Her Soul

I should have loved you like you said I said I would.
-- Rusty Johnson
I am doll parts.
-- Courtney Love

A saint dreamed she died and her soul
sailed invisible up to heaven where
it was nailed by thieves to an old oak.

And Robin Christ, that thief of thieves,
who begged for water and got piss instead,
leaned on the altar of her suffering,
giggled into her ear and said --
this theater of magic which is my body!
this bay of vinegar which is my blood!
take them and remember the horrors
I teased from under thy thumbnail
when I was a voodoo doll on the juju tree
and thou were queen of New Orleans!

And next, Romeo Christ, that whoremonger and slave,
who longed for true love and got the cock instead,
swaggered up to Saint Cassie
where she squirmed against the bark
and winked and spoke into her mouth --
swallow this.
She did.
Her throat rose like a sparrow to the tallest
limb where it sang a song of love and dread.

And then the Old Jackal Christ, that traitor and coward,
who wanted out and got sliced thru the ribs instead,
limped to her side and said --
where is the part of thee I desire?
Is it thy face or neck, between thy
legs or thy hands or ass or thighs?
Is it deep in thy body where
the Ripper searched with blade?

15

From Her cruel tree gentle Saint
Cassie sang this song to the Three --
you write songs about my
cunt but not about me.
I'm twenty-six dimensions
folded into four,
a fraction of a second after
creation, wheels within wheels,
a dream within a dream.
I'm the one that got away.

And They beat Their chest and cried together singing --
thou art the square root of minus one,
thou art quantum and curved,
the shadow universe
dreaming us into existence!
Thou art one fine bitch!
And thou art lost to me!

They gave her half of what she wanted.

From her velvet bonds on the satin tree
she smiled on the hapless One-In-Three.

An old saviour without cash is pathetique!

Shit
(written the day before Allen Ginsberg's death)

They're burnin' off now -- the dirt scag
machine gun narcotics I been suckin' down
for thirty-five years -- and the patient is hittin'
an all-time low.

I got freight train head
running full gear on red hot tracks down
the rail line of the ole spiney spine and those
spider-willies under the skinny skin, cut 'em
thin to win and I want some more shit
more than I want my woman or to go on suckin' air.
And it's gonna get worse and I Goddamn well know it.

Been tryin' to quit, playing Dylan and Lennon over and over,
tryin' to get back to when I was young,
tellin' myself anything to keep from makin' that call.
I'm walkin' the floor and shoutin' Ginsberg from memory
and poundin' my fists in my eyes.

Come on down here you baggy pants lotto big city asshole!
Come on down you young punk and see how life is!
Get pearl jammed up in the borrowed hallways of capitalism
then say fuck it to that
and jump back from the boardrooms of the overhip dollar,
start on the lifetime adventure of mighty fine love. Just like me.
I thought it was a gas, thought it was The Muse, thought
it was everything but what it was. I's havin' fun.

Slowin' down now, gettin' real sick. Make the call or die is what
my brain screams. I say look at these old hands and the wrinkles
on my face and the old-man's hair. I'm undesirable, gone but
somehow still here. Been Alicia Silverstoned! I'm ugly history.

17

But oh my friends I was graceful in my day, burnin' torch head
like some crazy bearded Statue Of Liberty. I burned and
burned and I'm blazin' this trail for you, you young fuckheads who
know every Goddamn thing in the bush-beck world. Look here! Look here!
Look here! Let my death be your roadmap!

Gardeners

those who never lifted earth
lift my son's body in its sleeping

whispered prayers can't hide
the open wound in his chest

but i have hidden seeds in the boy
so when he's planted in the ground

rebellion will push up
like some crazy crimson flower

Fanny-Min Becker

Kindheit

Zur Musik von Leslies Pink Floyd
Tanzt er auf dem Dach

In der Hand
Ein Raeucherstaebchen

Mit roten brennenden Kreisen
Bemalt er die dunkele Sommernacht

Unendliche Spiralen
Unendliche Kindheit

*

Childhood

To Leslie's Pink Floyd Music
He dances on the roof top

In his hand
A burning incense-stick

With red bright circles
He lights up the dark summer night

Endless spirals
Endless childhood

Paradise Found

in the east of eden
they bared their bodies
they took one bite
and re-entered paradise

A Told Untold Tale

Through the
Dark tunnel
Of an unforgettable past

She came

Flying into my dream
Halo on her head
Flapping her black wings

She came

And froze
My mother's last kiss
On my sweating forehead

*The setting is a convent in Germany during the Second World War. The
'she' is a nun running the convent. The 'I' is a little German girl being
sent to the convent together with her sisters. Their parents were occupied
with helping to smuggle Jewish artists out of the country.*

Eric Boutilier-Brown
Spiral Staircase, Fort Knox, ME
Photograph

Michael McNeilley

for grace

our small boat rises quiet with the tide -
the mooring tugs it in toward the shore.

tight ringlets dark, the color of first blood,
enough to coil around my fingertip.

light upon the water paints a line
of green across my hand, down your side.

I write this with my tongue upon your thigh:
there is nothing I can do about the moon.

billy's on the roof

billy's on the roof of the school again.
he's running around up there
like a wild animal.

we think he climbs the gutters
up to the top, though no one's
seen him do it.

the school psychologist
can't get him down.
he's done something to the door

at the top of the stairs this time.
he's locked it somehow.
it won't open.

he's throwing paper airplanes
all over the place
the playground is

littered with them.
some of them are his math papers.
mr. harris will be beside himself.

we think the gym teacher
will have to bring him down.
he says he'll find a way.

it looks like he's taken off
all his clothes.
better cancel recess.

Liz Haight

A State of Despair in Thirty-Seven Minutes

This night I drove east with a quarter tank of gas and no money.
Made a list of the places I could have stopped. I could have lain
in a field of goldenrod. Or drowned in the rain
of a crop sprinkler. Hung myself from the deadwood
of an unrisen barn. By the side of the road there is the ruin
of a genuine art deco trailer diner; I could have entered
between its halves. I might have stopped at the golf course
and sat on a bench against the hedges. Offered three grown men
sex on the porch of an antique shop. Or tangled myself
in idle farm machinery. I could have walked into the muck
of a quiet swimming hole. Coaxed a milking cow to smother me.
Closed my eyes. Where the road and the river
bend.

Valley Falls to Cambridge
NYS Routes 67 & 22

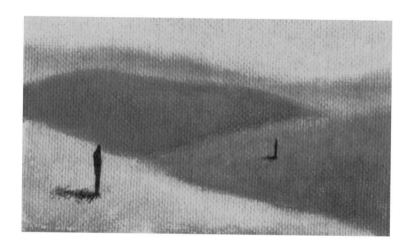

Lisa Marie Pecore
Voices
Acrylic on canvas

Suzanne Fortin

Anorexic

kneeling to the toilet
she offers a cornucopia

prays to be

desirable but untouchable
looked at but ignored

that she'll finally be able
to wear her rosaries
with padded cleavage

and tricks her hunger

the kewl

they descend like seagulls upon carre d'youville
infested-- plagued-- with suburban overkill

girls whose chests are illustrated with cannabis
spraypaint "fuck chretien" on the royal bank edifice
boys drink the latest from the microbrewery
sporting impudent nose and eyebrow jewelry

a man with an earring nods to "heart-shaped box"
as his partner curses televangelist flocks
i try to shut out the tabarnaks
watch the crosslight   avoid the bike racks   condemn them

for being so crass and lewd   forget
that it's only smug certitude   try to

drown out
            silence
                        the public mood

drown out
            silence
                        in solitude

NOTES:
        Carre d'Youville: [CA-ray DYOO-VILL]
a square in Quebec City where the marginal
types hang out.
        Chretien: Refers to Jean Chretien,
Prime Minister of Canada, whose surname
translates as "Christian".
        "Heart-Shaped Box": song by Nirvana.
        "Tabarnak" : [TAB-ber-NAK] A French
Canadian swear word; corruption of the French
word "tabernacle".

27

Krist Bronstad

Boy by Boy

My friend the ex-sniper
with a fake knee
has gotten used to sleeping with the light on
crawling through sleep like an infant through a burning house.
How unsettling
to wake and find your watery reflection
on the inside of a sliding door
in a retiree's house
near the Canadian border—
your colorless mouth gaping, slanted to one side
your hair a mess of muddy brown leaves.
And to tell us nothing
to collect your nightmares silently
like soldiers
lay them end to end
in the footlocker beside your
childhood bed.

My friend the ex-sniper
with the fake knee
stocking Batman toys from a
fifteen foot ladder
under flickering flourescent lights
eating lunches of canned soups alone
in the employee room
watching his co-workers
with finely cross-hatched vision
imagining them each separately
with mortal wounds
their innocent guts splattered
across the row of lockers where
pictures of fiancees wait to be adored
and civilian shoes wait to be worn
out into the cold Michigan day

My friend the ex-sniper
with the fake knee
once a lavish hotel room scenery eater
once a boy who was nothing but a boy,
in a smoking jacket, in bare feet,
in thin underwear, hanging his
jeans from the chandelier
tracing trip-heavy fingers across
velvet-pasted paisley wallpaper.
And a good shot too
and not a half bad liar
and it took what?
365 times 24 hours
to turn him into a camouflage flesh monkey
shooting hot metal pulp from
gum trees.

My friend the ex-sniper
with the fake knee
an imposing Northern shadow
self-styled, hulking gimp
tossing words at
girls in pancake make-up
up near the Canadian border--
man in the mackinaw vest - yeah, that's him
blunt features in the sunlight in the camera
in the swamps so early in the morning,
his boots so clean, so carpet-soled.

Joy Olivia Yourcenar

Iconolatry

We don't really want to know our muses.
Intimacy gnaws reality
and we bury the bones
in our shallow, unmarked collective unconscious.
Let the Mona Lisa keep her secrets.
What pressing need of prurience is satisfied
by knowing her teeth were bad
and her breath stank like rotten flesh?
Fleeting creatures of surface sensations,
we prefer not to know
the substance of our dreams.
Do not tell us
that the Venus di Milo,
the alabaster projection of desire
would have used her arms
to hold us at a distance.
Our petty personal mythologies
could not survive
revelations of flabby upper arms
and a nervous, self-inflicted manicure.
We love illusion
and we turn from our muses
when they show us
they are flesh and bone,
fear and foible.
Aesthetically bankrupt,
art offers us no absolution.
In the absence of grace,
we are reduced to icons.

Millay

I, being born a woman and harassed
must steal time
from my exponentially increasing
responsibilities
to write the rhymes I see.

I, being born a woman and overworked,
must remember cadences
amidst the concessions I make
to daily life,
seeking only time to savor.

I, being born a woman and mythologized,
must spread my working thighs
to give you pleasure
and me temporary respite
to dream of Camden in the summer.

Eric Boutilier-Brown
(untitled)
Photograph

Mark Hartenbach

sonny liston

could drop a mug
with one punch
but the drug
left him
with a taste
that he savored

it followed him
down to the mat
from a phantom right
to a fleabag hotel
singing
old sharecropper songs
rocking to the high
the sweet bye & bye

Jennifer Ley

Childhood Lessons

It rained yesterday, here in New Jersey
Torrents, buckets, cats, yes and little dogs, too
My husband discovered the encroaching footprint
of a water table filled to bursting
(no thirst here, all glasses full)
and ran to the basement, mop in hand
We tried at first to check the growing tide
Nature, over bountiful
But as the water level rose
(mere inches really, this was no biblical flood)
I remembered my childhood
and a house too close to a creek
the four feet of water that would rise
inexorably each spring
and how my Father and Mother
(after that first year, when they cursed,
as first time home buyers are wont to do)
calmly placed our basement things above the water's reach
knowing it would eventually ebb
And I said, darling, Let's not fight this
It's an unusually heavy rain
Let's just get our things off the floor
Here, give me that mop, silly
Let's go upstairs and do what people do
on rainy days like these
Let's spend the day in bed

This morning the basement was dry
The floor dusty, like old bones
It was I who had become wet
and full

Margaret

I put a bit of my Grandmother
her bread baked flour smell of safety
into my garden
She is that shaded wonder
white hearts waving along a supple stem

As the larger flowers fall
new ones swell to take their place
infinite as the summers I spent
wrapped in her easy soft bellied love

But the rabbits have eaten my poppies
so I'll have to buy seeds
for my own loaves
I hold the jar in my hand
and punch the dough down

Mike Barney

Singing the Silence

I

The woman on the Nicoderm commercial
was evilly baiting her companion:
"Come on, don't you feel like cheating?
Have just one!"
The companion, heroine of the piece
smugly declined, her
three-day abstinence
completely unthreatened.

Back in reality
my own 976-day truce with the weed
shaky as the Middle-East peace process
I turn off the TV
and take a cold shower.

II

You and I know
The Kama Sutra
is an owner's manual

The positions describe
required maintenance

So permit me
to dance
like a hypnotized chicken
while you peruse
the next-needed procedure.

III

Last New Year's Eve
I saw Kali
dancing wildly with some
young stud-muffin.

She was groping him
with her four hands--
he didn't mind!
while Shiva sat in a corner
watching, laughing, clapping
and counting out the minutes to midnight.
Looked like trouble brewing to me
so I lost consciousness
and faded from the scene.

IV

The wife says humans
have an obligation to die
after living out their time in full
of course.

The earth
she says
can hold just so many fools
at any given time.

The husband hears
murmurs noncommittally
as husbands do
mentally begins to redesign
his plans
for a
cryogenic storage chamber
to house one less.

V

Once
I spent an entire evening
alone with
Christ
trying to persuade Him
to teach me
how to perform
miracles.

He declined
politely
citing the
Messiah's Code of Professional Conduct
and certain
Magician's Union regulations.

We still had a really good time, though
sipping wine and
chatting about some of His more
famous stunts, like
the loaves and fishes bit
(a real crowd-pleaser, that one)
the Lazarus gag, and
the whole
crucifixion/resurrection/ascension sequence
which He told me
He'd later taught to Houdini
personally.

When the evening was through
I found that He'd
pulled a stunt on me--
disappearing all my tears
and turning my fears
to joy.

One hellava trick, that.

VI

Gaia, poet of the world
does not read her work aloud
but sings to herself
in the silence of creation.

Cheryl Hight Carle
Winter, Fairburn Georgia
Photograph

Peter Casey

The King of Grant Park

The King of Grant Park
Has no loyal subjects,
Unless one counts the trees.
Waving their fickle colors in the breeze.

He has no train of courtiers
Asking for dispensation of favors
It is he who asks, bleary-eyed,
for cigarettes,
pocket change,
food,
Or a joint.

Slow-witted tippers of ugly bottles say,
With liquor on their breath,
When the King sobers up,
He takes the bus to see his wife.

His Queen lets him bathe, change his clothes,
Sign over his government check,
Sleep in her bed.
They fuck and drink and argue.
Happy to be together
For a couple of days.

The King of Grant Park
For cash under the table
Stops kids from shooting each other,
Restores old houses,
Rescues dogs from Animal Control.

The kids he stops for free.

The King of Grant Park
sleeps under picnic pagodas
Smokes his dope on the porches of friends
And rises every morning higher than the sun.

Ruth Daigon

Under the Hammered Sky

schooled in flowers
matriculated in bombs
we're trapped in a common dark
under the bearded earth with it terrible cuttings
dreams suck us through night4242's keyhole
and winds blow ashes of yesterday
we learn the shape of dry space
and the liquid life below
dust swarms through gusts of quiet
as light congeals on the surface
no tears to scald the snow or melt the peaks
no sound except the squeaking of a prayer wheel
not a flicker is spared
not a funeral note
only the sea sucking on empty bottles

Not Yet Visible

My father balances on scaffolding
high above our games.
Each time he spits a nail
and drives it in
a wall goes up.
Room dividers rise
from hopscotch squares
the whole house framed on stilts.

He climbs the ladder
waves from every window
until I catch his signal
return it and find myself
waving from our top floor
at his bent frame growing smaller
as he moves along receding avenues.

I look out
signaling my sons
who for a moment
recognize me, signal back
then shift into a new position
straining to see something
not yet visible.

Chuck deVarennes

Lord Jesus Never Drove A Cadillac

Lord Jesus never drove a cadillac.
Nor begged the cash to build a golden tower.
We pray to you God, give us our faith back.

Hell-raising preachers thunder that they lack
Worldly wealth to increase heaven's power.
Lord Jesus never drove a cadillac.

The Lamb of God did not use prayer to crack
A cruel whip to make us kneel and cower.
We pray to you God, give us our faith back.

From ministers whose purpose is to pack
Collection plates each Sunday worship hour.
Lord Jesus never drove a cadillac.

Denunciations dim our souls to black
Remnants of spirits rendered hard and sour.
We pray to you God, give us our faith back.

Save us from evangelical attack!
Free our battered souls to rise and flower.
Lord Jesus never drove a cadillac.
We pray to you God, give us our faith back.

Under the Spell of "May Day Sermon"

In Gilmer County Georgia the women mourn by instinct.
They cry over deep memories of lovers who tore them
from their fathers in their dreams. Dreams Dickey divined.
Dreams which rolled through his mind and beat a Bible cadence
out through the lightning of his arm, screaming onto the pages.
The women mourn. They know him only in their dreaming possibilities,
only in   fantasies   of get away   of walking those woods and the faded welts
from their fathers, maddened by misused Bibles, cut for the glory of God.
They walk to the quarter moon's grinning challenge.   He has died,
their interpreter, their liberator, who thrust them onto the motorcycle seat.
Who told of the May sap rising, their involuntary ecstasies, their scourge
and resurrection and freedom. Now he's gone with them up the high trail,
through the straight brittle Georgia pines. He joins them in the dreaming
ecstasy of clouds. The always mystery of fogs. Fox skins flash back
from the barn nails. The whole farm moves toward his climbing spirit,
singer of scourged ecstatic girls, singer of blood in the bone, and sky fire.
He goes to join those swirling memories he transposed.
Some Gilmer County women may not read his verse,
but they feel his spirit in the trees,
in the skin-tearing willow branches of Gilmer County, that spirit
which sang their souls, made them free and immortal.

Lee Moskow

Burning in Common Time

she hangs her demons
on velvet ropes -
talks in rainbows,
smells like lilacs.
twenty years ago,
this would have been romantic
now I just look at
her forlorn face and
bloodshot eyes,
soft jazz in the background. she
summons charlie parker or
miles davis while I
stare
and remember when she walked
with demons,
hand in hand,
smoking unfiltered cigarettes
drinking gin straight up
and saying
"i love you."

Scott Murphy

Stalin, Dying

Save by the killings, these starvations,
how would I have created
a thing as terrible as silence,
the emptiness that swept to me
as I resolved to lead?

Prayer stained our knees
We knelt. God spiked us to the earth.
But I knew the absolution.
What other leader saw
how love and forgiveness
could best be kept apart?

I think I knew the number of the dead,
but my mind slips away.
Did I ever sleep?
Did I toil in the nights,
counting?

Hopeless now, I know I slept.
I cast off any rules.
Number seemed least of all.

My anger has burned through my breast.
I devised the death of the world:
death vandalizes me instead.
Finally,
I cannot hold it all.

Michael Hoerman

Eight Hour Pass

HH Highway is mystical
The Hog's exhaust reverberates off the hills
It returns to us like a cosmic secret
Buttoned down into sunset curves
We are stoned immaculate

The biker's jacket is black leather
It is worn and creased with many tragedies
By giving me a ride he's paying dues
This is not the first time
He's walking a paper tightrope
The real cutting edge makes men bleed
Somehow they wind up paying for the privilege

He's giving me a ride back to a big party
It is to celebrate my return home
I'm bringing the balloons

It happens in two parts
First, a thorough strip search
Second, a handful of laxatives
I sit on the toilet grunting
I am surrounded by customers
I am like a king holding court
They've been saving laxatives for a week
Everyone is delighted when I begin to shit

I retrieve the balloons out of the muddy water
Packs of smokes begin to exchange hands
Compliments are flying like curses
They aren't afraid to kiss my dirty ass

I think about the guy who drove me home
I hope he made it back to his own home
My home is the Jasper County Jail
I am safe and in great demand
His home is the real world
He is alone and in very real peril

Janet Buck

The Vapor Trail

Its path defined by looking in
and counting pennies in a jar.
A nickel for a stanza here.
A quarter for the thaw.

I'm selling syllables, I know.
Like Girl Scout cookies
at the door. The buzzer
louder every time the baggage
of an aching heart is dropped
like bombs from passing planes.

Jet streams of emotive skies.
The vapor trails of bleeding pens.
A treasure chest of coral reefs
that somehow pops its angry lid
and lands upon the page.

This is where the moonlight sings
and whispers something in my ear.
This is where I gather strength.
Relinquishing the need to use
the shoehorn of a stoic smile
to force my toes in normal shoes.

The long giraffes of wandering
through forests wet
with where I've been.
Introspection's porcupine.
It has a chance to cross the road.
This where I clean the gun
of coming home to me.

Lisa Marie Pecore
Rain
Sculpture

Dave Sloan

Dead Monkey Grows Cooler

Monkey fell through a hole in the sky
Exploded on the rocks right by my side
Held that beast to my chest with his body still warm but
Dead
Monkey grows cooler
Dead monkey grows cooler

Wound up crab come clacking his claws
Laughing hyena licking at his balls
Bats buzzards rats and worms
Gathering for the feast 'cause
Dead monkey grows cooler
Dead monkey grows cooler

Now I know I was a monkey
Way back when
I was seven years old
Hiding up in that tree
Uncle Bernie with his belt
Down there looking for me
The ground where I landed was rocks and roots
Dead monkey grows cooler
Dead monkey grows cooler

No crawling leaping creatures gonna eat this one
Dark deep and safe
You know I gotta bury him
So I take my belt and tie his neck
To a rusty truck hub
Throw 'em both in the ocean where
Dead monkey grows cooler
Dead monkey grows cooler

52

Still Trying

In third grade they said I was gifted
Gave me my own teacher
From that day I was alone
I walked from school
Kicking through piles of fallen leaves
Watched them fly
Dance, fall back into the gutter

I listened to the bells chime each day at three
They were not Church to me
I knew nothing of Church
The chiming
Carried across the sky
Through the outstretched tendrils of naked trees
To my solitary walking
And kicking
Connected me to the place of mystery
Where our yearnings were born
And where all loss resides

Energy is conserved
Nothing can be lost, utterly
Simply removed
To some other place
The place of mystery
Where loss lives in union
With the beauty of the chimes

Some bully came one day
This is my street
You can't walk this way
Anymore
I was afraid not to hit him
I had been taught
You let them run you off one street
They'll simply run you off the next

And this was the street
With fallen leaves
In piles cresting high above the gutters
And the chimes

I was frightened, he was stronger
He would get me eventually
Pretending to kick a rock
I crossed to the left side of him
Because I was left handed
And I did not want to miss

I did not miss

We fought even
He said things
And left
I tried to send the sickness of it
To the place with the chimes
And the loss

Today I heard them ringing
Carried across the grey, winter sky
Across the tops of small houses
Through the naked trees
I was taken to that place again
I saw the birthing of my dreams there
It was good
To see that boy dream
Of creating beauty
And know that thirty years later I still care enough to try
Of course I saw a lot of loss as well
Like you, I've seen so much of what I've loved
Removed to that place
The hardest thing, though
Harder than the loss of
Love's first tenderness
Harder than the loss of
Time

Ten thousand nights passed alone
Irretrievably lost
Harder
Was the sight
There in the place where all loss resides
Of that small left hand
Curled into a fist

CK Tower

Acquiescence

They say it is now winter in Michigan
though she can't remember when it wasn't.
The useless sun hangs well over the Tropic
of Capricorn: late afternoon suspended
in gray. A rush of dry arctic rustles the blinds
rattles the window: a sound like the sea roaring
against the glass.
Great Lakes splendor pales
in late October. Off a distant coast, southeast winds drift
seaward over southern Italy. But here the air is dusty
with old snow; she dreams Sirocco and steaming
Mediterranean.
Deep into midnight within the speechless
expanse of black, stars flash like bits of broken glass,
while the moon offers a sliver of conciliatory
illumination: a shred of bleached light paying
brief notice to a thousand blades of frozen
grass. An unexpected moment of elegance,
or a promise to the courageous:
one day she will cease waking to cold earth.

Breaching the Distance
for d-

"...half-changed into an elegy for all
  I'd known before, in candlesmoke."
                              -W. F. Lantry

The furnace bangs out a requiem mass
but these icy fingers tucked between thighs-
the last gracious repository, aren't wed
to the caprices of the metal hearth. While
breast knee and calf still serve, still peak
bend and flex through December's attenuated

hymn, memories of candlelight six hundred miles
and eight months anterior, resuscitate the song
in other joints surfaces and curves. Or a humid
voice rousing a body from mounds of silent
comfort at nine a.m., when nothing else
compels accelerated pulse through limbs. Except

perhaps the sonorous tones of sigh flash sigh
as we breach the distance, find passage
between golden stars. And lying
in a cleft of melodic symmetry, unleash
their milky rivers: an aria composed of duplicate
hunger-harmonies we've yet to sing aloud.

Carmen Butcher

A Season of Violence in Two Different States

And everything was greening, you said, and did not hear my wan bend hail great
tired dead happy fields between us. (Newness crying, milk ran, I was a buttered
breast.) You meant trees, shrubs, anything you saw sunk in the seat on the way
bumpy way back home from that strange place where you left left and right
breasts in exchange for calendars of clean tissue. And everything was
greening, you said -- not the assault on me midnight black and near-death
blue, not follow-up surgery shocking pink, emergency fluids and all drains
red, not endless tests made me white. And again, as if silence meant this
could maybe be beyond conception, you said, And everything was greening.
Well, I could not disagree then; smiling at the reclining inadequacies, I
cradled the phone closer to hear (I hardly knew who) saying gently, Yes.

Sweet Perdition
(for Christopher's Sixth Birthday)

)So
drink
drank
drunk

on honeysuckle   we
didn't let go of the spin   Drunk
on spinning   we didn't let go of the grass   Drunk
on the grass   we didn't let go of the moon   Drunk
on the moon   we lost our souls

happily   to the cow   the dish

and to the spoon(

59

Caron Andregg

Last One Up

The last one up wakes
to find the eggs already laid
tiptoes on sleepy feet
toward the swordplay of silverware
the quiet clash of knife on plate, wedding china
in a compromise pattern, already chipped.

Day breaks, conversation strains
floats in disconnected storm cells
above the breakfast table
fragile and transparent as Steuben glass
sputters to a stop among the yolk and shards
as we stumble from meal to meal.

Mirage

The house needs iron lungs
baked to the point of stroke
its airways collapsed

Electric fans resuscitate the night
with seared-feather draughts
cactus-dry

Adrift in this desert
we've forgotten how to breathe
each other's air

An ocean breeze
crashes and breaks
against mountains far to the west

I dive for deep water
the mirage on your molten skin
too hot to touch

You rise from between my thighs
sleek as a seal
your face wet

Air splashes time
against the wall of your chest
pressed like a shell to my ear

Through the night a black fan
turns and turns
and it sounds just like the sea.

It's Just Like Riding a Bicycle

Spent a week visiting old friends
Got a ride from the airport into town
Wet and cold. Not ten minutes back
And there's a beer in your hand
And a line on the mirror
Right off the pad and you're back in it
Jesus, were all your friends drug dealers?

The generous one sends you home with a gift
A rock like a monarch's lost jewel
She watches, aslant in the doorway
Loose-jointed while you weigh it
On a grain-scale stiff with disuse
Creamy-thighed and kittenish
As the coke-whore creeps up her legs.

It all rushes back so easily
Almost forgotten, but never quite
Just like riding a bicycle.
You start out saying you'll only snort up
On weekends, never on school nights
Then rationalize why this once will be okay
Not too much, just a pick-me-up
A toot between dinner and drinks
You know when to say when.

She found out you did a line without her
And hit the roof. Suddenly you saw it all
Unwinding, just like before; the witch-stranger
Standing aslant in the doorway
Of the house you put up your nose
And all that pretty weaponry
Always out, always loaded.

Better to back away now
While you still remember how
Afraid to hustle any more blow
Now the adrenaline rush
From the fear of '3 strikes'
Lasts longer than the high
Besides, your connections all wear
The faces of your best friends' kids
And you can't trust anyone under 30.

So you pour yourself another single-malt
And count the lives you have left
Put Big Brother on the CD player
Janis, digitally remastered
Sounding better than she ever did in life.

Dancing Bear

Sin

The gods do not see me
I am too small
for their eyes
even when I am not
trying to hide

Hunting Accident

We shot poor fucking Phil!

moving through tall autumn grass

- a deer among men

blurry-eyed men with high-powered rifles

bubbly burpy drunk on cheap beer

The Dreaming Poetry of Hydrogen

My dreams burning like Hindenburg zeppelins
in the cold gray morning
I rub hot ashes in my eyes
straining to cry for the loss of fantasy
I could be a painted witch-doctor   but
the minute hands of rain would wash
away the facade
Does this mask look good
I cannot tell
It was built from inside to out
Hydrogen is burning quicker
only the flaming skeleton remains
to come crashing down

In a room full of Gods
none shall fear my bones

Jolie Simmons
B&W, Lafayette Cemetery 1994
Photograph

Perry Sams

From a Line by James Wright

"I would lie to you
If I could."

I would tell you
America is
as beautiful
as that song.
I would tell you
about the bridges
stretching across
the Mississippi
the Hudson
the Colorado
a few miles
outside Las Vegas.
I would tell you
only of beauty queens
not beauty gone to seed.
I would mention Mount Rushmore
not Russell Means or Leonard Peltier.
I would laugh like a wild horse
steaming up a Nevada dawn
and not say how laughter
gets canned and sold.
I will tell you how Bob Dole
has the best health care
in the world, but also how
a woman with a shopping cart
holding her treasures
has ulcers swallowing
her bare feet,
and just so you know I'm lying;

after dark
she sleeps
with her eyes open
like a sunflower
standing outside your window.

John Coltrane and the New Cannibals

Marilyn was dead or dying
at this point, already
right up there on the screen
and the vicarious thrill
or itch around the spine
of seeing that,
Man,
so fans picked up on Trane
instead and he couldn't
go anywhere while he was
truly himself without someone
having to touch his coat
or finger his cheek
or kiss him and breath in
all the jazzbreath they could
get to mingle
with their own loneliness
Man, and somewhere in
bars lit only by candles
and the sound of the new savior
of music up on the--
wooden stage
there was a feast,
of lung and brain,
of tendons and eyebrows
and Trane getting thinner
and thinner until, like
Ralph Ellison sez,

Man, he
became invisible but not
in the same exact way--
It was almost funny
the fans doubled over
when they dragged him to the toilets
and chewed on bones,
and some fanatic saved and carved out a flute
from the thigh-bone

but by then it was too late to ask for autographs
so noone believes this story
but I was there
you were too, weren't you?

After the Blues, 2

"It is a green day."
Robert Creeley

This is why
I'm Robert Johnson's
natural child
why I write poems
like blues
like jazz
one fat note
following another
like green elk
bounding
through sleep
why the narrator
is never neutral
why a surf
of heartbeats
piles onto
the shore;

Because Bob Kaufmann
is dead,
Ginsberg is dead,
Bukowski long gone,
because I'm alive
because words
are bullets
at 3 am
because poems
shouldn't be
invisible
or wallpaper
or sacrificed
to some
sheepskin knives
all the time

Because Celan
left the camps
with poems
stuffed in his
pockets
because
Hart Crane
died worddrunk
and lonely,
because Viv Eliot
starved on silence

& because
I am
alive.

Julie Schillinger

Because They Have No Predators

there are too many deer in Ohio,
they say, some will starve,
stare into headlights causing accidents.
Caught in urban jungles,
jumping from parking decks.
Gunned down in the streets
by police like uncommon criminals.

I read this and think of you
out there in the woods
waiting for deer. Camouflaged
in your treestand, for hours
unable to smoke, holding back
three cups of coffee.
Unshaven, rising before dawn
showering, shampooing with deer soap,
hiking for miles through the wood
in boots sprayed with skunk urine.
Wearing long underwear, flannel,
and denim, activated charcoal-lined
hunting jacket.

Jolie Simmons

Sand

so busy with your
smokescreening,
your
beach-combing you
don't even see how I
freeze, I melt
the one large mosaic-me
the ivory-soap-it-floats of me
becomes
and becomes
smooth, egg-shaped stones of me
the kind that unthreatening sit in
gentle sand my
soft bare winter feet in early summer the
smooth, cool stones of me
Long Island quartz of me
catching light from either
way
half of me is ocean, half of me is
sky you don't realize I'm
there
you're not aware
waves of grief,
grains of lack and carelessness
grind me into grains of sand and smaller
smaller
and I am sun-warm quartz sand
cooling through your
fingers
bits of liquid, frozen bits of want
jingle-shells with thought and ought run out
most of me you cannot keep

no
matter how hard you try to hold, keep me
catch me
too tardy, you'll see
you'll see you'll
see me disappear through spaces too late to
help but like fleeting, fleeing, wanting
sand, a few
grains remain to
chafe.

You Are Salt and Seawater

you are salt and seawater
you are
an
unfinished sonnet,
a rhyme, a hum
between lips, a whistle between
crooked consonants a
whisper
tossed among velvet southerly verbs
a rush of water, whirlwind dervish of scented air
you are red skies at morning
and eyelashes that burn
in afternoon sun
you cause sirens take warning
like a netted, knotted veil over freckles and
blue-lined, blue-veined tender skin
you are scales that glint in
bitter water, cowlick spirals like
homes carried away
tendrils twisting secrets
around to
breathe in the
nearest ear.

Touch

Interesting how we may
touch
certain parts only
of ourselves of each
other

interesting
how we can walk the
wall between the land of
the living and the Province of the
Hesitant Friend--

Interesting.

Take the liver, for example:
I would love to touch your liver,
rest it in my hand, nibble
gently
so ladylike in claws and feathers

then there are my eyes, so
corruptible, so
pluckable
you kiss them from across the
room on your way to flies
and a fresh champagne.

Our hands are good - yes, let's
land there for a
watch-stopped moment.
Our fingers intertwine like
Ivy; each educated joint of organelle unafraid to touch
its fellows.

lips… are for riddles, questions,
quotes my lips are for me chewing on; I
taste my own blood between thoughts.

feet atouch are wonderful but
who thinks to do so?
A delicious waste, that

Forget the heart, though - at least mine -
at least yours. Mine is packed
in cotton-wool; yours-
well, yours is encased:
no touching, no leaning, no flash photography.

Karen Wurl

Third World Weekend: A History of This Disunited State

Prologue:
Succeed to this position, enough
rope to hang,
to be well-hung. Rob from the rich - who else?
Give to the poor and get
a receipt.
All my worldly goods
I thee endow.
Let me show you. This handful of you.
How tear ducts work.
Who wrote the book
of gravity and fell from grace.

1. Excluded from history, I was the continent
that lay in your path,
I was in the way
a land
mass. Your banners won't make me
go away, another occupied country,
domino down,
dissolve. You should see
the mark-up.
You won't doubt
the blue of my blood
once you taste it.

The conquerors always
come from heaven, angels,
blue-eyed, armed to the teeth.
They think rape's a favor,
I should be flattered.
They are panning for pearls
and mining for whiskey. They
know where to anchor.
What eminence to ascend,
what to take slave and what
to slaughter.
Their eyes are sick with beauty,
till sightless,
they barter spun cotton.
The nets in which they sleep
like pearls
are hammocks
are veils
are shrouds
and they, pale beings
divorced from heaven.

2. What alchemy
turns the milk to pus in your Anglo-Saxon veins? It must
be love
that makes us lean, till we rise
in the east and set without warning.
It must be love
that leaves us listless
inclining,
declining,
in decline,
this time.

In what river shall we drown tonight?
The stars are very
pretty here. They are not watching, will not see
you deny me with your arms around me.
They will not witness
the map of your possessions,
or shudder as a splendid policy of isolationism
falls before your advance.

3. Do you remember everything?
This cholera, sour taste,
buildings we
abandoned?

I am sick with self-
induced stupidity, still dream of being
dumb
enough.

You have ways of making me talk.
If only I had just one way to make you listen.

It wasn't a war, it was limited
engagement. We agreed it would never
be war. We agreed we would stop
in time. But we couldn't agree
when it was time to stop,
just that sometime,
somehow,
someone
ran out of bullets.

Oscar Wilde to Lord Alfred Douglas;
from his deathbed in exile

I guess it was all about Daddy; it always is
with boys, reptilian changelings beached in mid-
evolution. Half-formed for water and half-formed
for air, fully equipped for nothing - I don't
hold it against you. You were a pretty
jelly fish
a manta ray. Not some tadpole,
domestic
pet, no, I love
the vicious, exotic, your crippled
beauty, your fine
teeth,
the marks they made on me.

Still I dreamed
of better. I never thought
to march into hell alone; I thought I had your
affection. Its absence was hell enough. What shame, what grief
did you endure for me? What, for my sake,
did you renounce? Did you exchange
the work of a lifetime, hard-earned respect,
for a cell, or for this
poor room, separate by an ocean's width
from all I knew of life? Did nothing inside you
shatter? I am

broken
they say; what do they
know of the word? Of any word, of Language, my former
God, the one I cast off to serve you. Yourself a literary
conceit, a device; I couldn't have penned
this tragedy without you, my classical
demise, my fatal flaw, you siren, you suicide, my
hubris made flesh, you gorgeous chalice of hemlock, exquisite toxin.
Each man kills the thing he loves -
unless it kills him first.

You, child, how could I
corrupt you? who were so spoiled already, rotten as fermenting
fruit? I was drunk
on your petulance; and I wanted to be
that blind, I was tired of seeing. Did we only
play at love? If it was a game, the stakes
were high. I always covered
your debts, defended your honor. I still do. Here is my last
installment,
what passes for will and testament.

My dear, I am indicted still
by my own folly; still remember the silk of you
draped upon me, more
than ornamental. I still remember hands and breath.
And I would crucify myself afresh, die ten more lonely deaths,
all to hear you murmur once again,
my name draw itself from your throat
like it was all the benediction
man could ask for.

in Joe's case, I knew

Leslie,
I'm kidding myself.
It's not as if my attraction to him were
emotional attraction
But hell,
he could go for me, too

Since Joe, who I loved,
Steve who I dated last year,
I have, yes, made plans with him
we have a lot in common
another meaningless though not unpleasurable fuck.

now that I'm falling in love with George,
he thinks very highly of me as a writer
in spite of what we said
the gut-level trepidation I felt about Joe
I think we could be
pedophilic
suffocating each other

after our fling on his office carpet,
it could be an indication of interest.
I don't feel
this alive
George and I could be lovers,
he does call, looks to be wanting
university freshmen.

He's young, he's beautiful, he's passionate,
that doesn't automatically translate.
Never had anything but
regret falling in love, and in this case,
here I am exhibiting all the symptoms

he's a grown-up, man, he's a man, he's of age,
I didn't like his poetry enough to sleep with him twice, I think.

we chatted and have since exchanged
curiousity and lukewarm feelings
autobiography

thinking that maybe
he's a romantic
he wasn't going to love me back.
he's a good writer,
close without
acquaintance
asking me out again.

The thing is, I have not seen the guy who used to come to the poetry readings.
Throw the rest of me at him as well
like I loved him; I don't.
I think we could happen to each other.

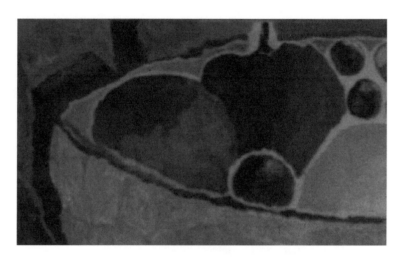

Cheryl Hight Carle
Fruit IV
Acrylic on canvas

Shari Diane Willadson

VA Beach Roomies

She has marked all the eggs
with the word "mine"
in grease pencil.
Forgetting once again
that we had saved her
when we buried her stash
by the third set of steps
that led to the beach
after her boyfriend had called
saying the pigs were coming.

We went back later
and dug in the sand for hours
maybe the second set of stairs?
She told old lady landlord
about my snakes under the bed
and I cried as I kissed them goodbye.

The three of us
on a Saturday night
giggling into a blue-eyed dawn
dropping quarters in the slot
at strategic moments
in the hard-dick comedies
while thin, sad men
with messy hands
play musical booths.

then a walk on the beach,
we smoked a bowl
of the yellow carpet fiber
you bought on the boardwalk
thinking it was Columbian Gold
and we were sick for a week.

I don't know where
you two are now
but Susan, I'm still mad
about my goddamn snakes
(your stash was under the FIRST set of steps)
and Pat?
I never did sleep with Owen,
he just wanted to make
you jealous.

Mass

From down here
it looks like
you are right
I was missing
the point.

Of course
your shoe
on my chest
makes the truth
very clear.

I'm not fighting
laying here
is soothing
with the earth
at my back.

I can't stand
on my own
anymore
anyway
you know.

My gravity
has exceeded
my mass
even without
your shoe.

So what if
we see
what happens
take a step
away
will I fly?

Please Stand By
(published in *Gravity* as "tech time")

Until you cut that rope, there is no saying
how many buildings you could jump
or marshmallows you could eat.

What I mean is,

who really cares about the dress out weight
or fat ratio of Japanese beef
as compared to, say, Carolina chickens?

What I should have said was,

how do you propose to make a living
with your husband gone, two kids on drugs,
taxes due, and a dirty oven?

No that's not right,

Carol is still pregnant by her rapist
and considering birthing half of the sextuplets,
and giving the other half to charity.

So really, who's to say?

When the world ends, the only things
Sally takes comfort in are daddy's rolex,
summer camp, and her whitening toothpaste.

dissection has two s's

it wasn't the roadkill
that bothered me much
it was dead
past knowing
thirst
or want of a mate
i objected to
the classes
sweaty-palmed boys
looking on the insides
with steamy glasses
giggling, pre-pube chimes
prodding
the vessels of life
making faces
sharing disgust
over the internal
things that soon
they would worship
turning quickly
on their heels
to embrace
the unembraceable
expecting
a smile
in return

Looking in a Mirror Out

She was selling potholders
outside the supermarket
I picked a blue one
with uneven stitches
some kind of white flower
crocheted in the middle.
She said I wasn't old enough
to know if I was crazy yet
but that I would know
before anyone else told me
like looking in a mirror,
looking in a mirror
looking in a mirror,
looking out.
There wouldn't be one thing
I could do about it
but it would be best
to be by a river
when it happened
because water is so much softer
than concrete
and washes away
most of the stains.

spark

Behemoth Rising

I surface now,
piss-water slipping off my slick skin
shiny like stars.

You shoot away
as fast as your slobbering little engines
can swim you.

Across the waves,
scintillant and gleaming black
I spit at you.

You are horrified--
This is my sea, yellow and stinking
and I am all your ancient fear.

Diving, I return
the toilet world's ocean bottomless
anal and sludged.

Cast off, you.
Grab your shit-filled catch;
I am below, and you know

that deep and underneath
there is only darkness
and true terror.

Life in Antiquity

On the morning of my birth
an Archangel came within my sight
she spoke to me
and the sand opened up beneath my mother.

The forests grew gray as I dawdled
The trees were laden with shadow
The exactitude of the brook
betrayed by late summer.

Now the winds of winter
ruffle me, and
I am childless: Guilty
in the quick darkness of the evening.

Michael Brackney

Tommy From the Coast Remembered
(for an old man on the street)

I've been on this street
a while...since Johnson.
What'd Johnson say -
"they're all my helicopters"
girls work this track never kiss
never kiss

had a lot of money back then
I was young
a lot of money
Me and Tommy drove past
the cadillac ranch
past New Mexico
to the LBJ ranch
I'm talking L B J
the big Kahuna back then, brother
to the front gate

The suits said, What's your name
what's your name!
Tommy From The Coast
he said and just walked   just   walked

gotta get some coffee
sit down have a rest - have a talk
they don't let me in some places
'round here 'cause they know
who I am, you know   who   I   am

When Tommy was here we had the run
of this street, man
the whole town, whole   town
they took Tommy and locked him up
locked him up   somehwere
dangerous, you know   locked him up
From this street straight to
who knows where - come for me some day
they like a clean street
clean street
He must've died in there
'cause dead folks don't come back
and Tommy wouldn't leave here without
me

William Burns

Osiris on Fatherhood

I tell you Isis
   that boy is going to be
      the death of me

Raven's Day at the Shore

She
Looking out to sea
    electric blue dolphins vaulting
    in her hair

Grey-Green
Oceanic eyes
    cresting over me
Engulfing my every thought

One with the coming tide
Soft
Gentle
Unstoppable

River Dump

The gutted yester-dream cars
   lay on their sides
   like trophy-shot dinosaurs on display.

The scavenger rats scuttle about
   rattle tink, rattle rattle tink tink....
They fear that if the moon rises
   they will have to hide.
   Such are the rumors of rats.

The moon rises on shiny hubcaps.
It's OK,
   as moon rises go....

The rats scatter.
They will be back in a short while,
   it doesn't matter.

I can see the river now.
It trudges through the trash,
   like an impotent old man
   who thinks he's doing the world some big favor.

Over there between two cars,
   a couple of daffodils bloom.
I walk over to look at them.
 I startle a rat,
   Sorry....

There is only one daffodil.
The other is a piece of yellow plastic,
   it doesn't matter,
   at a distance it's hard to tell.

They are OK,
   as daffodils go.

David Donlon

Elvis in Hell

Elvis will never die. His star will not go out.
We could go into the Dionysian aspect of his forced
Resurrection, or the Christian, the Tammuzian, the
    Osirian.
We can look at it from any fixed point, draw any
    conclusion.
But men are not good gods.

                    In every house
Across America Elvis is genius to someone.
We want greatness. It was so giving of him
To desire to be great, was it not?
How much more to linger.

"Elvis Saves Old Lady from Path of Bus"

He still walks among us. He has
Been spotted at a gas station in Albuquerque.
He waves to the ladies, shyly. He guides souls
To heaven. Heaven + Elvis = Helvis!
He looked inside and found an abyss.
Put it off awhile; sing, swing the pelvis
For the swooning crowd.
For a while.

Elvis is in hell.

If you tell me he hung on a cross, I'll believe you
But he made no ascension;
Only the dark-star's
Endless, inward declension.

96

A Spirit of Solitude on 14th Street

The night is not damned. It is the only thing that is not damned
Because out of it we make what we please.
-William Carlos Williams

Tell me the meaning, what meaning there is
In the bright sun seen out of a kitchen
Window, refracted through glass, while the drip-
Dripping of the faucet gives time it's edge;
Or in the world turning away from the sun
As it has ever done Sunday evenings,
Or tell me what meaning there is in my
Insistence on Sunday evenings and then
We have started. I have heard it said that
Now is the pleasant, the cool, the quiet
Though not silent hour before the moon
In its full orbed power fills the landscape with
The reflected light, and with highlighted
Shadow takes off the mask of things. The
Shadows will all grow to a length in their
Hour; see, they know it, and will not cease
Their encroach. Yet the light finds surfaces
To gleam upon; this light that shines and gives form
And color to noon, but fades into deep
And deeper grays at twilight; this light
That warms our sense and brings the knower
To the known. Light is time.

II

I watch the shadows grow vital and long,
The light flees to higher and higher ground
Until at last the mountains cut it off
From it's source, and it seeps along the
Streets, in retreat, circling about the lightpoles
Coming on. Dark's army, incorporeal,
And mortal, is marching -- soon entrenched
All along Madison Avenue.

                             it
Is quiet. A few souls in pairs, voices
Lost in the miasmal dark, are out, going
To or away from some more brightly lit,
More vivid existence. Ah! Suck the shadowy
Air awhile into your lungs, breathe it thick!
Oh waywards -- if you did not send out such
Lights of your own how the night would change you!
Can you feel the livid weight of life
Penetrated where you wrap it, shell like
In form?

                       I am a connoisseur of darks,
And this is my resume, so see:
I have tasted the dew laden gusts of
Spring evenings, drank in a hot Hattiesburg
Night, the air molten and thick with water;
I have savored the cool, dry edge of
Phoenix at dawn, and tasted the moonlit
Pacific salt of dark rocks and gleaming foam.
All these darks unique and unrepeatable, yes, but
The air at night is always absolute.

III

The sweet hot odor of asphalt is rising;
A seductive gust blows boxwood. Grass and
Cat's piss mingle, waft, and tease the nose; then,
More boxwood. A door slams. I recall
A gloomy night, years ago, when I thought
About the mystery of dark -- when, in
A motor-boat on the river, its
engine cracking and spitting like some
Phlegmatic miser threatening to cut
His losses and simply die, we heard,
Between the bouts of cursing, before
The sparking motor coughed, behind the
Whisper of wind, a silence we all know
Along the waterway; the soundless dark,

Thick and obvious. With no preamble
Somehow the motor caught. The sudden swift
Motion! The night! It obliterated
The river. Only the wind on our faces
And a few distant lights served as our link
To boundaries. We were at one with the
Whirl of Chaos; at one with timeless dark.
This, I thought, *is something.* When I felt
My wet grip on the gunwale I had no proof
Of more to my reality than my fingers, nose
Heart and cloying tongue. Had I toppled back
Would the smooth water have enveloped me
With the caress of divinity? Do you know?
Because, as in caves, I sensed that prior
Divinity, entombed and forgot beneath
Human thought, like that we sense where ancient
Men rendered on cavern walls shapes of
Errorless grace. Now that is something.
Primal caves. Smoke and pigment in the dark.
Beasts long since recalled into the dreamworld.
Whose fingers? With what art? Such a subtle wonder
Inhabits those forms that their eternal charge
Haunts us still. We ought to fear them like gods.

IV

This city changes in darkness, but not
So you would notice. Follow the wind, as
Drunken revelers careen, laughing, past
The all night deli. The wind swirls
In the murky street, across from the
Darkened buildings of the University,
Which stand resolute, forbidding,
Absolutely, any legal entrance into
Their domain. (There is that army
From before, standing guard upon the door.)
Can night-knowledge be so despised?
But let them sleep. Nights as these, whether marked
By us or not, have ever passed, are passing

And will pass, in some eternal moment.
Look, there's a rat, sniffling and worrying,
How he slinks along the gutter so quiet
And low; that is his emergent ratness.
Just so have all rats crept to the crypt of
Permanence. What? Now I am reeling!
I have lost my balance here, suggesting
Forms are tombs! Now that is *really* something.
But let it pass -- Let our rat vanish in
The night and hope he meets a lucky end,
Or by god's grace let the *cat* be lucky.

For what are we but vibrations on a string,
Wrapped, loose or tight, around a tubed membrane?
Have we eleven dimensions? Or ten?
I will go ask the mathematician
For my new world view, and he will say,
'Today it appears that our vibrations
Are in *n* dimensions, not particles
Glued together, mind you, as we supposed,
But *vibrations* -- it is illusion,
A trick of the light, which gives rise to form.'
Ah, but the Buddha told us that before.
In time the mathematician will change
His mind, or seem to, in the fresh light
Of new evidence, and with his words make
New worlds; such power has his poetry,
For time is but one of his dimensions,
And is pliable in his wizard hands.

Then have we now reversed St. John, and flesh
Become words, defined now loose, now tight?
But the professor of Deconstruction
Bids me think that words are nothing alone,
Until they take their supplements. I say
Do the math; well fed words, then, will we be,
By the old law 'Ye shall be what ye eat.'

Oh, the night is damned all right, and we are
Lucky enough to hold our forms against
Such onslaughts as these we nightly suffer.

V

Strings of silver boxes snake their way
From east to west and back again, hooting
In the night like lovelorn, plaintive owls -- when,
Where, why do they go? Chugga-chugging oil
Slick silver snakes, like *clockwork, on* time, or
Just off, or *very* late -- yet on time enough
For us to know the hour. Late, very late.
I remember reading, or seeing on
Some indolent midnight-oil burning
Production, shown during those hours which
The blissfully benumbed never know, yet
The fitful, *uneasy-awake* know and
Count among their living moments as time
Spent *away* from the cause of unease and
Therefore as time *well* spent -- where was I now?
The train. There was a circus train, back in
The days of circuses, when the t.v.
Hadn't yet been discovered as the best
Benumber, Nineteen and Twenty-nine, to
Be exact, in Bloomington Illinois;
A *terrible* accident. The animals
Screamed in the night -- the elephant's legs were
Smashed, and she lay on her side heaving until
The sheriff shot her in his mercy. The bear
Blinded, rambled through the quaint suburban
Countryside, confused and moaning, too hurt
To live until the dawn. The strongman joined
Her in death, whimpering his own chorus
Of pain. Some say they *still* hear the whimpers
And moans on foggy nights while the air is
Thick and windless. Yet why would they linger?
What force on this earth could make them stay?

You ghosts -- you stay beyond your hour,
Expecting something -- I see you testing the
Rails for signals that never come; I see
You standing dumbly while the cars of
Other days flash and burn by your shadows.
I really do see them, here, on this street
For my mind has called them, and here is where
All crushed spirits return when called, here, out
Of the light they gather around me, formless
And begging.

_____ We do not fear the dead. It
Is the changing life within us, the wheel
revolving, charging along the tracks, lights
Illuminating unknown terrors ahead,
The snapping jaws of oblivion behind,
And strange shades falling by on either side.
We do not fear the dead, for they reside
Only in our memories, locked in our
Conceptions, and powerless. We fear the
Pregnant maw of formlessness and oblivion.
It is the shadows . . . *the shadows* . . . they catch the
Eye.
_____ *My* how the streetlights sway in this wind.

VI

Hush now, be still. I hear a voice singing
Sweet urgings in the wind, out in the dark:
When you acknowledge me, on that day I
Will sing; I will sing to the skies, and they
Will sing to the earth, and the earth will sing
To the plants of the field, and they will sing
To every living thing. It is the song
Of eternity, the song of kinship.
The song is real and it is holy.

We must not profane it with our faithless
Talking. But then what shall we do?

Now here comes the town drunk (or one of them)
Like Lear he staggers in his disbelief;
Unsupported, naked, outcast -- martyr
To his own woe. He intends, I think, to
Sleep somewhere on that wide green lawn, up the
Dark hill. He is determined to do it.
I have seen him roll half the night into
A heap on the sidewalk, marking it as
His own. He crawls up to his feet, needing
Something the night possesses, something up
The hill. I have never seen a man so
Determined. Leave him free to complete his
Design? No, he never had designs. He
Is an empty vessel, and some other
Power either fills him and tips him
Into mysterious cups, or leaves him
Thus empty, sick, alone. Blame whichever
God you choose. The bum blames booze.

VII

At last the stillness I love best descends:
Here is where the moment begins; the time
That really counts, out here in the dark
Among the sounds and smells, where you can still
See the wavey whorls of chaos creeping
When you look down the long, deserted street.
This is Gödell's law. The frame is shown cracked
At every edge; we are not so well contained
As we had hoped. Forms waver on the brink.
To be here is a dicey business. Here
Is some eternal essence, where order
Meets its edge and a decision is reached
About the boundary. And every night
It's the same argument -- the same play of
Forces. How can anyone know what keeps
The sun's light coming? Who can guarantee

103

The morning? I shudder against the cool
Brick wall on 14th street and feel my clothes
Moisten with dew, eternally patient.
Who, Me? No. The cloth. The brick. The dew.

VIII

The forces begin to grow restless.
With the sun waiting around the world's edge,
Here is where the battle will be pitched
As the minions of darkness make their last
Stand against the light. The glowy troops
Around the light poles, nearly vanquished,
With their last strength revive and receive their
Succor from the eastern tint. The minions
Swirl in confusion, tear their frocks and steal
Back into recesses in dismay and
Disorder. They go sliding down storm
Sewers, into the boles of trees, and under
Bellies of low, crawling things. Oh, how beaten!
How dispersed! What the moon oversaw
As fair victory, in time turns
With the sun's coming, and shadows
Fall to become slaves of the quick.
All the will has gone out the night.
At last the morning gloom begins, and night
Is lifted; the troops march back into
The foothills, and guard close the walls. No more
Voices are heard, or have been for hours
Except for the hushing swish of wind
And thrum of passing cars. It is time again.

IX

At last we return from our all night vigil,
Back to the drip, dripping faucet, back to
Cheap linoleum and cracked drywall,
To see the sallow light reflecting through

The window, as the world spins us in

Time again. The day brightens. See! The light
Shines on us and we are full of holes, full
Of shadows; nothing can penetrate us
That has not already. We and the night
Are one, as unfinished around the edges,
As sticky about boundaries. No edge
Is sealed for ever. No form an Ideal.
Yet my edge is sealed. Ha ! For the moment.
That is just a pithy thought, a template
for some grander design it will not fit.
Our idea of completeness is the culprit,
For the complex will never admit it.
The set of all meanings remains -- in spite
Of what logic, what system, what mind
Attempts to rule -- undefined. What comes to
Light, what is grasped, what achieves consciousness
Will ever be a bounded circle in
An infinite field. The mathematician
On the hill knows this: No formal system
Remains complete; contradictions are wove
Into the seams -- it is method is the
Stuff of dreams. *Now that is really something.*
Out the window I am looking for the bum,
To see what he has become, because it
Makes every difference. The university sits
In its daylight splendor, and there he is
Snoring under an elm, still a minion
Of the dark after all this time. But the
Light, given chance, will crack him like a seed.
What was never well contained will then spill
Out again, and at last he will be more
Than anyone's designs can describe -- which
Is, I have no doubt, what he always was.

Lisa Marie Pecore
Source
Acrylic on wood

Lisa Marie Pecore
Homage
Acrylic on wood

Amy Wright

Hunters and Gatherers

i.

I really should allow myself more space, she thinks,
scribbling another haiku. Uncross my legs, unpocket
my hands, breathe deeply. It's the fault of those
Crosswords, their symmetry.

Running her finger around the rim of a heavy Pfaltzsraff
plate, Janine recalls breaking things, un/doing. Her mandolin,
a witness, splintered in a pink shoebox on her closet shelf.

   ::

Her wig is matted, tucked between her panties
and rose-scented soaps. She places her head in the kitchen sink,
squints as the water rolls down her forehead. Maybe
I'll be a shampoo girl, she says, her voice hollow against
the stainless steel. After work, lay my neck in the basin's collar
bone.

   ::

Mornings always take a little too long. With teeth brushed,
she eyes the newspaper, waiting impatiently. 8:37.
Three minutes allotted to walk to the Bridge Street train.

   ::

In the plexiglass
she mouths her best words:
street light, subway, ivory.

ii.

Kenny Jamison puts on his shoes
one shoe at a time.
Sock, shoe.
Sock, shoe,
leaving one foot bare
while he ties the laces.

This trait is newly acquired.
Months ago he would have
stepped gingerly on rain drops.

I have overcome
my table of contents, he says
to no one in particular.

iii.

Nora collects
broken safety rings.

She claims synthesis as their appeal.
But really, it is their resemblance
to the smooth shells of locusts
that allow them to pile up in her drawer.

Joy Reid

My Claim

Tata,
don't evade me,
make hump back shoulders,
walk away.
Pride was always your
favourite child,
but I have a claim as well.

Tata,
look at me
I have your eyes,
blue as icebergs
trapped beneath the surface.
I have your height,
your thin, fine hair.
Look at my hands
broad as shovels
unlovely, but capable,
wide feet too,
aeons of
splay-footed peasants
are recorded in my feet.

Tata,
forgive me,
I know this brings you pain,
but you see
I am so frightened,
so ashamed
of what I'm asking,
I want you so much
to love me,
once before your death.

Philip Havey

Overleaf

If page five, where the dying child plugs into the roll
Of her mother's hip is held up to a strong light,
The woman leans against the wall of gold
From the story on the next page about the U.S. Mint.
Positioned in an inset box, high within the bleedthrough,
The Secretary of the Treasury's ghosted face averts
From both mother and child, his wire-rimmed glasses
Riding school-marm like down the thin dorsum
Of his nose as if just receiving an improper answer.
The precious metal glitters through the greasy paper,
Dominating the date palms and foliage of Bangladesh;
The pustules of the child on our side of the page fester
Like birdshot wounds against the unblemished bullion;
By accident or design, both the man and the woman
Find a common focal point to right and off the page
With an equally shared disinterest for time and place,
As the child dies another consolidated column inch
Within the stapled binding of a magazine called - "Life".

J. Kevin Wolfe

van Gogh Says

van Gogh says to God "I do not like
your gawky use of trees in your landscapes so
I made my own.

You make the starry night breathe
but do not show the dynamics except
for in creeping shadows of leaves.

You pottered a flawless conch shell
a billion years ago but

what were you doing during post impressionism?"

Rochelle Randel

Concert Crowd

Weaving through the crowd,
A drunken boy - he way high, man.
Way high.
He want girl and woo her,
By rolling one eye,
One way,
the other eye,
Somewhere else.
Wide smiles at sky,
At ground,
Even directed to girl
sometime,
Like teeth beacon.
She also high,
Gone.
Seeing no burdens
to her pain.
She see only boy,
She not see future,
Or even present,
together,
They sink,
Sink into ground,
Into crowd,
Into earth,
waking later,
and later.

John Carle

Rain
for CHC

pain penetrates
me drop
by drop
-Sappho

　　　　here I am   take off my shirt
my body in candlelight slopes smoothly
　　　into thin denim   my skin

warm against the cold metal of buttons
　　　　my arms and ringed fingers
　　　want to be a river passing through you
how long till you come home   how much longer

to wait to make love to you   if you were here
　　　I would sing you my pain song   I would
　　　　sing you the wine song

the finger song
　　　the smoky kiss song
　　　　the sex-cry song
　　　　　the moon song

if you were here I would push the candle
　　　　into the wall   watch the flame
　　　rise mad to the ceiling

and outside   the rain washing down   the sky
　　　is echoing your thunder and oh my jeans
　　　　slap my body like your hungry tongue

Cheryl Hight Carle
Texture Study, Oakland Cemetery, Atlanta
Photograph

Jolie Simmons
BTW. Bridge, Fairmont, West Virginia 1993
Photograph

Ray Heinrich

after the last accident

i meant to tell you
after the last accident
with all those pictures
of the car and
the curled-up chrome
not wanting to look
cause you'd be
looking for blood
when the sound
of walking on glass
has you seeing
them again
and that white car
bent in the middle
on that trip out west

cancer

hard to mention cancer
lightly
politely

if you open your mouth
the death's head
might pop out

jesus from el salvador

jesus from el salvador is cleaning buildings
and tonight
he's in my office
vacuuming and emptying the waste baskets
and he's making money
and paying taxes
and because of the federal debt
his payroll deduction this friday
is just now going to pay
for the training
of the police
that tortured
and killed
his wife
and two children

how far away it was

i'm standing over my father
in the hospital
he's stopped breathing
i'm holding his neck
and shoulder
and i've been rubbing them
because he always liked that
and it's the best i can do
while i'm waiting for him to die

waiting for his next breath

and it comes

and another

and then

i'm waiting for his next breath again

and i count

one thousand and one
one thousand and two
one thousand and three

like he taught me
standing in our garage
watching a thunderstorm
on the gulf coast of texas
sometime
when i was maybe six
he taught me to count
between the lightning flash and the thunder
taught me to figure out
how far away it was

Biographies

Caron Andregg lives and writes in Southern California. She has authored three chapbooks; *Dangerous Curves, Pavlov's Mistress* and *Of Chemistry and Voodoo*. Her poems appear in several literary magazines. She is also a regular featured poet at venues around Los Angeles, Orange County and the US, including the Austin International Poetry Festival.

Mike Barney writes: I practice law in Michigan, write because I must (either that or suicide) and have been widely but shallowly published in a variety of obscure magazines, both print and on-line (which almost always cease publication shortly after my stuff has appeared) such as *The Blue Review, JavaSnob Review, Vent*, and *Furry Chiclets*.

Fanny-Min Becker, British Chinese turned German. Living in Duesseldorf, Germany, with trade-developing husband and internet-developing son. Lover of what life has to offer, devoted wife, mother of three and more, friend, home-maker, teacher, writing/reading fan, student, roughly in that order.

Eric Boutilier-Brown, a professional fine art photographer, lives in Nova Scotia, Canada, with his partner, the poet Joy Yourcenar. He attended the Nova Scotia College of Art and Design, and has been pursuing fine art photography since 1991. His work focuses upon the Nude and the Ruin and since 1995 he has exhibited his work online at http://www.collideascope.com/ebb

Michael Brackney writes: After moderate success in writing "post-college" I woke up one morning to find out I was an accountant and hadn't written in sixteen years. I've been writing for a few months, having some poems and a short story in a handful of web-zines. "Tommy..." is a 'persona poem;' I love dialogue and speech patterns, and use 'persona poems' to create other voices.

Krist Bronstad writes: I'm a 21 year old lesbian who ended up in Lincoln, Nebraska, where I take care of other people's animals, make all jobs temporary, try to decide 3 years too late where to go to college, and write in a windowless closet behind the refrigerator.

Janet Buck teaches writing and literature at the college level and has published poetry in a wide variety of e-zines, journals, and anthologies. "Introspection's porcupine is an odd creature that comes in every shape and size. The tangled roots of mine are whetted by the rains of being born disabled. I have spent most of my life using stoic pride to squeeze what toes I had and didn't have into the brutal shoe of normalcy. Poetry, for me, is a tuba in a long parade that chases sorrow and pain to its dissolution.

William Burns (Millennium Artist) phased into existence in Washington DC circa early 1950's putting him on the trailing edge to the beautiful people of the late sixties. Bill is a strange confluence of degreed Electrical and Biomedical Engineer, graphic artist, actor, playwright, poet, father and husband, but his first love is poetry (OK, the kids are more important than poetry, but it runs a close second). I am calling for a balance between Art and Engineering, Rhyme and Reason, Yin and Yang. Other than that I like to hike, act in plays and drive on the Blueridge Parkway.

Carmen Butcher writes: I have a Ph.D. but don't hold it against me. I grew up near Atlanta and studied at The University of Georgia. I was a Fulbright Scholar in London ten years ago studying Anglo-Saxon. Now I'm a stay-at-home mother in Northern California. I chase my daughter, play with my husband, edit books, and write (revise) poetry and hate to cook.

Cheryl Hight Carle, when not working her regular nine-to-five job, paints and works in her garden in Atlanta, where she lives with her husband, stepdog and maladjusted cat.

John Carle is a writer and educator in Atlanta. His creative writing and articles have appeared in *Poets, Artists & Madmen*, *Perihelion*, *Poetry Cafe* and elsewhere. He edits and publishes *Gravity*.

Ruth Daigon was editor of *Poets On:* for twenty years until it ceased publication. She won "The Eve of St. Agnes Award (Negative Capability) 1993. Her poems have been widely published: *Shenandoah*, *Negative Capability*, *Poet & Critic*, *Kansas Quarterly*, *Alaska Quarterly*, *Atlanta Review*, *Poet Lore*, *Tikkun*. Internet "E" zines include *Ariga*, *Crania*, *Cross Connect*, *Zuzu's Petals*, *Switched On Gutenberg*.... also Poet-Of-The-Month on The University of Chile's *Pares Cum Paribus* (an "E" chapbook in English and Spanish). Her latest poetry collection is *Between One Future And The Next* (Papier-Mache Press) 1995. *About A Year* (Small Poetry Press in 1996), Gale Research published her autobiography in their Contemporary Authors Autobiography Series, 1997 and she has just won the Ann Stanford Poetry Prize, 1997 (University of Southern California).

Dancing Bear (dancingbear@rocketmail.com) is of Chippewa and Swedish ancestry. He lives in San Jose, CA. His poems have been published in many journals and magazines including: *New York Quarterly*, *Zuzu's Petals Quarterly*, *Slipstream*, *Poetry Motel* and *The Rio Grande Review*. He is a editor of several books and chapbooks. His latest chapbook is *Disjointed Constellations*.

Chuck deVarennes was born in 1954 (the year Elvis released HOUND DOG) in Needham Massachusettes. Grew up in Atlanta suburbs, intending to become the next William Kunstler. Attended University of Georgia on a debating scholarship, which he quickly abandoned (along with the rest of his academic work) to study brain chemistry through personal experimentation. Surviving, he has worked in commercial construction for many years, and is the happy father of one daughter. He has published poems locally, has performed spoken word on local radio, and can be found at coffee houses and other venues spewing verse.

David B. Donlon is a poet living in Alexandria, Virginia, whose work can be further sampled at http://www.erols.com/frmst1.htm.

Suzanne Fortin lives in Quebec City, Canada and is the editor of *Minerva*, a Catholic e-zine.

Liz Haight writes: I am the mother of two lovely daughters. Occasionally a poem happens.

Mark Hartenbach writes: I'm new to the Web but old to the small press. I've appeared in *Chiron Review, Black Moon, Bullhead, Fuel, Rio Grande Review* & many others. I publish *Wooden Head Review* and am grand poobah of non compos mentis press now in 3rd year.

Philip Havey says of himself: I was born an only child to an Irish Catholic family on June 29, 1930. This is important to know because I have spent considerable time being both American Irish and rogue Catholic...Like a figure eternally tap-dancing down the Yellow Brick Road Dorothy's shoulder, I have often come very close, not to perfection, but to being "truly human" without ever crossing over from excellent execution to art.

Ray Heinrich is an ex-Texas technofreak and hippie-socialist wannabe who writes poems for thrills and attention. Over the years his work has appeared in many small, insignificant publications. In real life he repairs computers, has always been married, loves dogs, and owns a blue fish.

Michael Hoerman, age 29, lives and writes in the Missouri Ozarks. In June 1997 the Missouri Arts Council awarded Hoerman a grant to publish PORTABLE PLATEAU: JOURNAL OF THE OZARK WRITER, which included new work by Tess Gallagher and Ginny Stanford, reprints of work by Langston Hughes and Frank Stanford, and Miller Williams' 1997 Clinton inaugural poem "Of History and Hope," as well as poems and prose by dozens of other Ozark writers. Hoerman was artist-in-residence at Spiva Center for the Arts in Joplin, Missouri from May-December 1997.

Jennifer Ley is an active member of the NYC poetry circuit. Her work has been published in *Excursus, Salonika, Perceptions, Minotaur*, etc. and is currently part of Grist on Line #8. She edits the hypertext site *The Astrophysicist's Tango Partner Speaks*, which is at http://www.geocities.com/SoHo/6115/. Hypertext poetry and graphics.

More than 300 poems and stories by Michael McNeilley have appeared in publications including *Mississippi Review, New York Quarterly, Poet, New Delta Review, Red Dancefloor, Hyphen, Chicago Review, Minotaur, Slipstream, Poetry Motel, Stet, Lilliput Review, Bouillabaisse, Impetus, Plazm, Writers' Forum, Rockford Review, xib, Exquisite Corpse* and elsewhere, including websites worldwide. McNeilley is editor of the *Olympia Review* and the *Zero City Poetry Website* (http://www.cruzio.com/~zerocity/).

Lee Moskow is currently undertaking a B.A. in Psychology. His poetry has appeared or will be appearing in over thirty journals, including Eclectica and The Black Bear Review. He is also Editor of two ezines, *Papyrus* and *Zen Rubies*. His work has been mainly influenced by Charles Bukowski and Samuel Taylor Coleridge.

Scott Murphy writes: I keep or am kept by a cat in Denver. Of the two of us, only I can open the little tins of foul smelling dish, so I believe I have the upper hand. When the sun shines I write computer programs, though it frustrates me that computers are remarkably intolerant of missspellings. (How many esses ARE there in mispell!?) I am forty-something, once attended the University of Colorado to no particular effect, and lacking a gas oven, am forced to consider myself either happy or crisp.

Lisa Marie Pecore is a 29 year old self-taught artist. When not studying art or practicing "serious" painting she works professionally as a freelance muralist and finisher in the Atlanta area. The rest of her time is spent renovating the old farm where she and her boyfriend live, along with 9 dogs, 3 cats and a parrot.

Rochelle Randel writes: To earn my bread, I work as a Marketing Assistant at a computer security company in Columbia, MD. To feed my soul, I've been writing poetry and short fiction for more years than I care to count. I'm actively involved in HeartSong Connection, a Baltimore women's group who through celebration and experimental group sessions explore issues of inner growth to rediscover the divine in life.

Joy Reid writes: I have had an extensive number of poems and short stories accepted by electronic magazines (60 poems in twenty two e-zines) this year and won prizes in nine competitions. I have also been selected as one of twenty four poets nation wide taking place in a ten day New Poets seminar in January run by 'Island'/ 'Scarp' and the University of Woolongong. I have also a novel, 'Serpent Call' which has been offered a publication contract by Northernlights Publishing, a Canadian company.

Perry Sams writes: Journalism degree, English minor, 1980. Wrote sports, courts, cops, music, features. Got canned, staggered sideways into poetry, got into Arizona art-scene early '80s. Have worked carnival, factory, cabs, convenience-store clerk, temps, library, bookstore and foodservice since to support my writing jones.

Julie Schillinger is a secretary for a chemical company in northeast Ohio. A hand-ful of her poems have been published in various e-zines on the web and small poetry journals. Julie often non-verbally communicates with her cat.

Jolie Simmons was born under an auspicious sign in June 1967, the summer of love, the day peace was declared from the Six Day War, and has been trying to remedy an incomplete education ever since. A native of Long Island, she most recently finds herself living in Atlanta, by way of West Virginia and D.C.; she plans to live in many, many more places. Both blessed and cursed a Gemini, she writes, designs, photographs, illustrates, prints, sings… and reads everything she can get her hands on. Jolie wrote her first poem at the age of four, has been writing all her life and was published a fair amount when she was much younger but then stopped showing her work for several years. Upon the closing of her twenties, she is pleased to discover a new writer within her psyche and has been stretching her wings and fingers furiously since. She is a core member of The Usual Suspects, an Atlanta-based writers' group, co-producer and -publisher of *The Usual Suspects Meet Frankenstein* and producer and publisher of the upcoming *Bride of The Usual Suspects* (both are book & audiobook sets). The latest in a long tradition of late bloomers, she plans to live a long life as it may take a while for her to find time for everything. She hopes to be catching a nap sometime soon.

Dave Sloan suffers from a horrific disease known to neurologists as Exploding Brain Syndrome. EBS cannot be cured. The final explosion can, however, be kept at bay by the crafting of at least one decent poem per year. Dave is endeav-oring to stave off the inevitable for as long as possible.

spark (Mark M. Sparkman) is a Utah-based writer whose work has seen oodles of publication and for which he has been paid very nearly nothing. He is large, bearded, myopic, lecherous and has your name tattooed on his butt.

Perry Thompson was born in Georgia in 1950. He graduated from high school in 1966. Two years running he was awarded first place in Columbia University's Gold Circle Award For Poetry for which he received a nice letter. He holds no college degrees. Mr. Thompson has been previously published in *Columbia Review, Dekalb Literary Arts Journal, Lonesome Virgin* and *Chattahoochee hReview*. A civil rights and anti-war activist during the '60s, Mr. Thompson has been handcuffed, spit on, hosed down, beaten up and generally abused by his fellow Americans. He currently resides in Key West with his wife, Marsha, and their cats, Bramble and Midnight and is the proprietor of Rainy Day Records.

CK Tower resides in Lansing, Michigan and attends Michigan State University, where she is continuing her studies in creative writing and literature. CK is very involved in the internet literary scene, as editor for *Conspire Poetry Journal*, and poetry editor for *Recursive Angel*. CK is continually working to provide useful, top-quality resources, to assist readers and artists in their literary pursuits. Some of the journals where her work as appeared include: *CrossConnect, The Allegheny Review, The Mississippi Review, Zuzu's Petals, Poetry Cafe, The Astro Pages,* and *The Morpo Review.*

Shari Diane Willadson has been writing for over twenty years.She has been published in *The Astrophycist's Tango Partner Speaks, Moonshade* magazine, *Poetry Cafe*, and *Poetry* magazine. She lives in Washington state, USA with her husband and daughter.

J. Kevin Wolfe writes: I write and talk too much. I write and sidekick for the nationally syndicated Weekly Rear View Radio Show. I co-host the regionally syndicated "Everybody's Cooking" on public radio. My fourth cookbook is in the works. I just completed editing and retranslating (with the author) the war diary of a 12-year-old Bosnian poet (published in two languages in Europe and being typeset for US publication.) When I grow up wanna to be a poet; a journalist for the soul.

Amy Wright writes: I graduated from the University of Virginia with a B.A. in English and am currently doing web work in Washington, D.C.

Karen Wurl is a dramatist, poet and songwriter. While awaiting film stardom and marriage to a series of Oscar®-nominated actors, she studies Theatre and Speech at Kennesaw State University, and works part-time in a video store. Miss Wurl has a small but rabid cult following (consisting of at least four people); her further ravings may be found at http://www.mindspring.com/~ophelia and http://pigseye.kennesaw.edu/~kwurl/. Contrary to rumors she may have started herself, she does not really mind being known as a confessional poet.

Joy Olivia Yourcenar writes: I am a poet, teacher, mother, technical writer and spoken word DJ presently living in Halifax, Nova Scotia. If I am writing, the door of my bedroom is closed and there is a sign on it that reads, "Before you knock, ask yourself, 'Am I on fire? Am I bleeding?' If the answer to both of these questions is no, DON'T KNOCK!" My children, amazingly enough, are both young writers. I collaborate with Eric Boutilier-Brown, my muse and life-partner, on a visual poetry website, icon/graphy, that combines my imagery with his photographic images. There is more poetry on my website, Mythologies. The best way to get to know me is through my poetry.

Errata

Peter Casey's biography should read: Peter Casey is a free spirit and jaded idealist. He is currently in disguise as a computer programmer.

Liz Haight's biography should read: Liz Haight is the mother of two lovely daughters in flight. Her venue is upstate New York. She has poetry appearing in issues of Agnieszka's Dowry, the 1999 Poetry Calendar, and several independent anthologies.

Page 7: Caron Andregg's poem is "**It's** Just Like Riding a Bicycle"

Page 9: The title of Cheryl Carle's photo is "Texture Study, Oakland Cemetery, Atlanta"

Pages 9 and 116: The title of Jolie Simmons' photo is "**B&W;** Bridge, Fairmont, West Virginia, 1993"

Conspire has moved to **http://www.conspire.org**

The "**4242**" on line five of Ruth Daigon's "Under the Hammered Sky" is extraneous.